Fact Finders®

AMERICAN INDIAN LIFE

The Iroquois

The Past and Present of the Haudenosaunee

by Danielle Smith-Llera

Consultant:
Brett Barker, PhD
Associate Professor of History
University of Wisconsin–Marathon County

CAPSTONE PRESS
a capstone imprint

Fact Finders Books are published by Capstone Press,
1710 Roe Crest Drive, North Mankato, Minnesota 56003
www.capstonepub.com

Library of Congress Cataloging-in-Publication Data
Smith-Llera, Danielle, 1971-
The Iroquois : the past and present of the Haudenosaunee /
by Danielle Smith-Llera.
  pages cm. — (Fact finders. American Indian life)
  Includes bibliographical references and index.
  Summary: "Explains Iroquois history and highlights Iroquois life in
modern society"—Provided by publisher.
  ISBN 978-1-4914-4993-6 (library binding)
  ISBN 978-1-4914-5005-5 (paperback)
  ISBN 978-1-4914-5009-3 (ebook pdf)
  1. Iroquois Indians—History—Juvenile literature. 2. Iroquois Indians—
Social life and customs—Juvenile literature. I. Title.
  E99.I7S62 2016
  974.7004'9755—dc23   2015009635

Editorial Credits
Catherine Neitge, editor; Tracy Davies McCabe, designer;
Svetlana Zhurkin, media researcher; Kathy McColley, production specialist

Source Notes
Page 28, line 4: Haudenosaunee Thanksgiving Address. http://www.nmai.
si.edu/environment/pdf/01_02_Thanksgiving_Address.pdf. 13 April 2015.

Photo Credits
Alamy: MixPix, 23, Philip Scalia, 4–5 (front), 26; Corbis, 21; Getty Images:
Photo Researchers, 25 (front), Stock Montage, 10; Granger, NYC, 6, 25
(back); iStockphoto: HultonArchive, cover (top), 1; National Geographic
Creative: Jack Unruh, 5 (back); Newscom: Photoshot/World Pictures/Tim
Larsen-Collinge, cover (bottom right), Zuma Press/Miguel Juarez Lugo, 17;
North Wind Picture Archives, 12, NativeStock, 27, 28; Shutterstock: Alexey
Borodin, 20 (front), Arina P. Habich, 20 (back), Brian Lasenby, 11, 29, Ewa
Studio, cover (bottom left), Keith McIntyre, 19, SF photo, 9; Svetlana
Zhurkin, 15, 22; XNR Productions, 18

Table of Contents

Giving Thanks

Every morning and afternoon, soft voices recite a prayer in Iroquois community classrooms. Speaking in native languages, they give thanks to all of nature—for plants, animals, people, water, stars, and sunshine. The children might feel thankful for strawberries they ate for a snack. They might remember the butterfly on the playground. They might feel thankful for a teacher's help.

Iroquois ancestors have passed this thanksgiving prayer down through thousands of years. The Iroquois weave their history and traditions into every part of their lives today.

ancestor: family member who lived a long time ago

tradition: custom, idea, or belief passed down through time

An illustration depicts the prayer of thanksgiving.

Chapter 1

Life Before European Contact

An engraving from the early 1700s illustrates the Peacemaker speaking to members of the five tribes, urging them to work together.

For more than 4,000 years, Iroquois tribes have lived in what is today upper New York State and Ontario, Canada. The Mohawk, Onondaga, Oneida, Cayuga, and Seneca tribes lived near each other and spoke similar languages. But they also fought bloody wars against each other.

Today the Iroquois tell the story of a man called the Peacemaker. He convinced the five tribes to work together as a **confederacy**. He showed them how a bundle of arrows was more difficult to break than a single one.

The Peacemaker introduced the Great Law of Peace. He urged the five tribes to solve problems without fighting. The tribes organized themselves into the League of Nations, possibly as early as 1142 or 1451. In the early 1700s the Tuscarora Nation became the sixth tribe to join the confederacy.

confederacy: union of people or groups with a common goal

The Iroquois today call themselves by the name their ancestors used. Haudenosaunee (pronounced hoe-duh-no-SHOW-nee) means "people of the longhouse." They constructed these houses out of wooden poles and covered them with bark. The buildings had curved roofs and could be up to 200 feet (61 meters) long.

Usually about 60 Haudenosaunee family members slept and cooked in their longhouse. Their extended family was made up of mothers, fathers, sisters, brothers, grandparents, aunts, uncles, and cousins. The extended family was called a clan. Members of the same clan considered each other brothers and sisters. They did not marry someone from their own clan. Each clan was named after an animal, such as a bear, wolf, turtle, or hawk. The clan animal decorated the outside of the longhouse and even the bodies of clan members as tattoos.

A reconstructed Haudenosaunee longhouse near Toronto, Ontario

THE LONGHOUSE THEN AND NOW

Until the 1790s longhouses were the center of Haudenosaunee family life. Clan members used nearly every bit of space inside the windowless, narrow buildings. They stored dried beans in containers made from tree bark. They hung dried corn, meat, and healing plants from the ceiling. They slept on cornhusk mats on platforms.

Today Haudenosaunee construct one special longhouse in each community. No one lives inside. Instead of beds, long benches stretch along the walls. Wood stoves have replaced fire pits. People gather inside for ceremonies and community celebrations. They sit to watch and sing. Or they dance in the center to the rhythms of water drums and cow horn rattles.

POWERFUL WOMEN

Women had great power inside the longhouse.
An old, wise woman, known as the clan mother, made
all important decisions inside the longhouse. After a
marriage a husband went to live with his wife's clan.
Haudenosaunee babies were born into their mothers' clans.

Men were leaders in the village. But the clan mothers
chose the young men who would become the chiefs and
their advisers. A chief's clan mother could take away his
power by symbolically removing his antler crown.
She might do this if the chief was not a wise leader.

Clan members shared tasks in the villages.

The clans worked together in each village. They often built wooden walls around the village but inside there were no locked doors. One longhouse in each village was a special gathering place. Inside, the chief, advisers, and people in the village discussed issues affecting them. Members of each Haudenosaunee village worked together to survive. Women farmed and shared their crops of the "three sisters"— corn, beans, and squash. Each plant helps the other plants grow. Men shared fish and the deer, turkey, and bear they hunted.

The Iroquois Confederacy worked together to defend its members. They defeated other tribes that were fighting alone. Together they expanded their territory from Canada all the way to Kentucky. The Haudenosaunee cared deeply about keeping peace between their nations. Each nation selected chiefs to represent each clan. The chiefs from each nation met in a grand council to discuss problems until everyone agreed on a solution.

Unity symbol

A pine tree became the symbol of the unity of the nations within the confederacy. Under the symbolic tree's branches members of all tribes were welcome to come to talk—and avoid war.

Chapter 2

Haudenosaunee Life Changes

Onondaga and British soldiers met around a council fire.

European explorers dramatically changed the lives of the Haudenosaunee. They traveled down rivers into Haudenosaunee lands in the 1600s. They searched for animal furs. Fur was expensive and fashionable to wear in Europe. The Iroquois nations hunted beavers for the Dutch and British. They eagerly traded furs for European cloth, glass beads, steel tools, spears—and guns. The well-armed and well-organized Haudenosaunee now won more territory from other tribes.

In the mid-1700s France and Great Britain pulled the Haudenosaunee into their war. In the forests of North America, the Haudenosaunee fought alongside British soldiers in the French and Indian War. Together they defeated France. But British colonists and American Indian tribes were still at war over land. Great Britain wanted peace with its ally the Haudenosaunee. King George III declared in 1763 that no Europeans were allowed to move west onto Haudenosaunee land. But the king's words could not stop the stream of British settlers moving west. The Haudenosaunee sold many of their lands to the British. They hoped that in return, the British would respect the borders around the Haudenosaunee Confederacy.

Deadly diseases

In the 1600s trade with Europeans caused the deaths of many Haudenosaunee. Europeans carried smallpox, measles, and other diseases across the Atlantic Ocean. The diseases killed more than half the Haudenosaunee.

ally: person, group, or country that helps and supports another

WAR DIVIDES CONFEDERACY

American colonists fought a war for independence against Great Britain from 1775 to 1783. The Revolutionary War started another war inside the Haudenosaunee Confederacy. Some Mohawk, Seneca, Onondaga, and Cayuga warriors sided with Great Britain. Most Tuscarora and Oneida fought alongside the Americans. Warriors now faced each other in battle for the first time in centuries, splitting the great confederacy.

During the war Americans and their allies killed many Haudenosaunee and burned their villages and fields. After the Americans won the war, they were still angry with the Haudenosaunee who had helped the British. Some Haudenosaunee fled north to live in Canada. Others stayed in New York. But soon they lost most of their lands to American settlers. The new United States was growing and its citizens were hungry for more land to build houses, roads, and railroads.

Once the Haudenosaunee lived in longhouses. Now they had to build new homes. Once they lived in villages connected by foot trails. Now they lived in communities scattered across two countries. But the Haudenosaunee today remember the confederacy's pine tree. They still feel their roots stretching back to their ancestors and history.

RECORDING HISTORY WITH BEADS

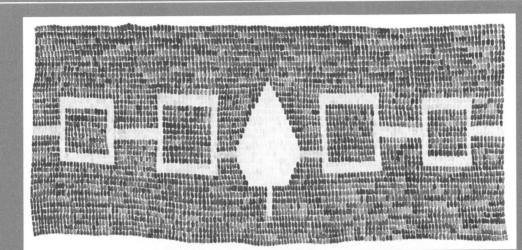

An artist's interpretation of the Hiawatha belt, which symbolizes the unity of the five original nations. The Tuscarora Nation joined the confederacy later.

Early Haudenosaunee treasured purple and white beads carved from shell. They were called wampum. Haudenosaunee sewed them together into belts, which were a form of writing. The shapes and patterns made by the beads recorded stories, laws, and history for members of the confederacy, present and future.

One famous wampum belt was named after Hiawatha , the Peacemaker's helper. It tells the story of the birth of the Haudenosaunee Confederacy. A row of white beads connects four white squares and a pine tree shape.

The squares and tree stand for the five original nations joined under the Great Law of Peace. The purple and white flag of the Haudenosaunee Confederacy bears this wampum design today.

Wampum belts were exchanged to mark treaties. The Two Row Wampum treaty of 1613 established formal relations between the Haudenosaunee and the Dutch. The two sides agreed to respect each other's way of life. After the British took over from the Dutch in New York a series of treaties and meetings continued. It was called the Covenant Chain.

Chapter 3

Haudenosaunee Life Today

The Haudenosaunee gave up most of their homelands more than 200 years ago. But they have not given up their rights as a people. In fact, in 1924 they rejected the U.S. citizenship act that made citizens of all U.S.-born American Indians. Some Haudenosaunee today consider themselves only citizens of their own nation. They issue their own passports. The Haudenosaunee live throughout the world including on territories and reservations in the states of New York, Oklahoma, and Wisconsin and in communities in North Carolina. They also live on territories and reserves in the Canadian provinces of Ontario and Quebec.

There are about 80,000 to 100,000 Haudenosaunee in the United States and Canada. The territories on which they live can be as large as thousands of acres or as small as 32 acres (13 hectares). Only one reserve—the Six Nations of the Grand River Territory—is home to members of all six nations of the Haudenosaunee Confederacy. More than 12,000 Haudenosaunee live at Six Nations in Ontario, Canada.

But many Haudenosaunee are frustrated with the borders of their territories. They have not forgotten the homelands their ancestors gave up after the American Revolution. They are trying to gain back their land through the U.S. court system.

Haudenosaunee today are proud of their nation—and their clans. They sometimes include their clan symbol in their signature. Clan members today do not share a longhouse. But they share names with their clan. Each clan mother keeps a collection of names used by her clan for thousands of years. When a clan member dies, she takes back the name for a future newborn in her clan.

The Onondaga are trying to reclaim land taken in violation of a 1794 treaty. The wampum belt (below) was commissioned by President Washington.

HAUDENOSAUNEE GOVERNMENT

Like Haudenosaunee villages long ago, each Haudenosaunee community has its own government. Sometimes it is elected and sometimes it is traditional. In the traditional government, clan mothers in each nation still choose chiefs from each clan. If the chiefs do not act wisely or responsibly, clan mothers remove them from power.

Legend:
- Iroquois lands at time of European contact
- Present-day Iroquois Reservations (Cayuga, Mohawk, Oneida, Onondaga, Seneca, Tuscarora; not shown, Seneca-Cayuga Tribe of Oklahoma)

Haudenosaunee communities are mostly in the North.

These small traditional governments still work together. Sometimes serious matters affect all nations of the confederacy. Forty-nine chiefs from all six nations gather in a Grand Council. The chiefs meet where their ancestors did—Onondaga Nation in New York. They also meet in Six Nations of the Grand River Territory in Ontario.

The Grand Council still follows the advice of the Peacemaker, who is the 50th chief and whose title remains vacant. The chiefs gather around a fire. They spend hours—even days—discussing problems. The discussions end only when everyone agrees to a decision. When they cannot agree, they collect more information and meet again.

The Haudenosaunee also follow U.S. and Canadian laws. And they are proud that the Haudenosaunee government is one of the earliest examples of a democracy.

INSPIRING THE FOUNDING FATHERS

Haudenosaunee are proud of similarities between the U.S. government and their own. When the Founding Fathers shaped the new American government, they could look at the Haudenosaunee for ideas.

Americans elect a responsible and knowledgeable person to lead the United States as president, just as clan mothers select responsible and knowledgeable chiefs to serve on the Grand Council.

Both the U.S. House and the Senate must agree on new laws. In the Grand Council, the Mohawk, Onondaga, and Seneca are called the Elder Brothers. The Oneida and Cayuga are called the Younger Brothers. Both groups must agree on decisions.

The U.S. Supreme Court decides if U.S. laws are in accordance with the Constitution. Haudenosaunee clan mothers decide if chiefs are acting wisely.

Chapter 4

Connecting to the Past

Haudenosaunee today hope to help their children grow up knowing their old ways of life. Like their ancestors, Haudenosaunee give thanks to nature for its gifts. Nearly every month of the year, they gather to celebrate foods that nourished their ancestors. As the seasons change, they prepare sweets or soups with strawberries, corn, and maple syrup— sometimes from their own gardens.

Haudenosaunee have always believed that plants hold powerful medicine. If Haudenosaunee have a wound or infection, they might go to the home of a healer. These men and women collect plants to cure illness. They learned how from their elders, who today still teach young people. They learn to say a prayer of thanks to a plant before harvesting its leaves or berries for medicine.

elder: older person whose experience makes him or her a leader

Like their ancestors, Haudenosaunee healers carve frightening wooden masks to scare away the bad spirits that they believe can cause illness. Selling or exhibiting the treasured masks is against the law of the Haudenosaunee Confederacy.

WORK

Many of today's Haudenosaunee have jobs that connect them to their ancestors' lives. In the 1880s some Haudenosaunee men moved to large cities to help build skyscrapers. They worked with steel at terrifying heights. They helped build many structures, including the Empire State Building. Haudenosaunee still do this work today.

Haudenosaunee helped build skyscrapers.

Because of their jobs, many Haudenosaunee now live far from tribal lands. Others live on or near tribal communities. They work as storytellers or teachers in tribal schools. They work in tribal government offices or medical facilities. They work in shops or museums owned by their nation. Like other Americans and Canadians, they have jobs in a wide range of fields.

21

CLOTHING

Many years ago Haudenosaunee replaced their soft, leather clothing with European wool and cotton cloth. But they did not forget their history. For hundreds of years, they continued to use porcupine quills and shells to decorate their clothing.

Haudenosaunee wear modern clothing styles. But at weddings, graduations, and other events, they wear traditional outfits. For such occasions both men and women wear leggings and moccasins. Their ancestors wore them to keep warm and to protect their legs and feet from the rocks and thorns of the forest.

Men wear loose shirts decorated with ribbons and an apronlike covering. Women wear dresses and skirts made of cloth or leather. Shell decorations remind them of early ancestors living along rivers. Silver and glass beads remind them of later ancestors who sewed European-made beads onto their clothing.

Gustoweh

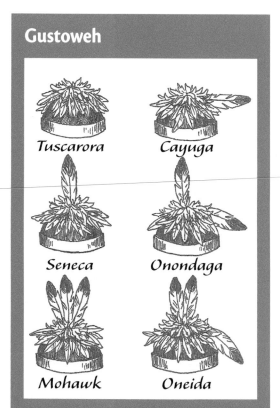

Tuscarora Cayuga

Seneca Onondaga

Mohawk Oneida

Haudenosaunee men wear caps called *gustoweh* decorated with hawk, pheasant, or turkey feathers at special community events. The number and position of eagle feathers in their caps shows if they are members of the original five tribes of Mohawk, Seneca, Oneida, Cayuga, or Onondaga. Members of the Tuscarora do not add eagle feathers.

The Haudenosaunee tell stories through dance.

Haudenosaunee wear their traditional clothes at powwows. They perform their fast-paced Smoke Dance for audiences of other tribe members and guests. Long ago Haudenosaunee men danced to prepare for war. Today women also perform the dance, spinning and stomping to a drumbeat.

EDUCATION

School buses carry many Haudenosaunee children to classrooms. But long ago longhouses and forests were their classrooms. The Haudenosaunee believe schools help their children learn their history and be proud of it. They remember how their ancestors suffered in schools from the 1880s to the 1930s. They had to cut their long hair. They were punished if they did not speak English. The Haudenosaunee hope their descendants will always remember their tribal languages. Some Haudenosaunee children attending public school take classes in their history and language.

Haudenosaunee run their own schools too. Students study math and writing. But they also learn to speak and write the languages of the Haudenosaunee Confederacy. Some students attend immersion schools where they speak and write only in native languages.

Haudenosaunee elders take great joy in hearing young people speak their tribal languages. It gives them hope that Haudenosaunee ways will live on.

SPORTS

Lacrosse is a popular sport among the Haudenosaunee. They run in teams, swinging long sticks topped with netted baskets. They dive after a small rubber ball, hoping to scoop and toss it into the goal.

Their ancestors also played lacrosse, but with deerskin balls and hand-carved wooden sticks. When early Haudenosaunee played lacrosse, it was much more than a game. Matches helped end arguments between people and tribes. They also believed playing lacrosse was like medicine and kept the community healthy. The game was like a prayer to honor their creator. Today Haudenosaunee men and women compete against lacrosse teams from countries around the world.

Lacrosse is still played with netted sticks and balls.

HANDCRAFTS

For the Haudenosaunee today, objects made by their ancestors' hands are part of their history. They run their own museums to teach their people and visitors about their history.

Haudenosaunee today also teach their children how to make handcrafts—just as their parents taught them. Their **artisans** today work with both traditional and new materials and tools, using their history for inspiration.

For centuries Haudenosaunee artisans have turned handfuls of tiny beads into works of art. Usually mothers have shown this skill to daughters. Artisans sew together beads of bone, shell, stones, glass, metal, and plastic—beads from various times of their history.

artisan: skilled worker, especially one whose occupation requires hand skill

Haudenosaunee might wear jewelry and clothing beaded with clan animals or a popular football team's logo. Some special beaded clothing is brand new. Other clothing is passed down from ancestors.

Haudenosaunee artisans have not forgotten the traditional ways to weave baskets out of grass and wood. They often use tools passed down from ancestors. Their able fingers can also turn colorful, factory-made plastic cord into firm baskets.

Haudenosaunee today also use new technology. They record elders speaking. They hope Haudenosaunee audiences will learn more about their history and others will learn more about Haudenosaunee life.

Beadwork and a birchbark basket display fine craftsmanship.

The Haudenosaunee are grateful for their long history. They believe their traditions make their lives more meaningful today. When they say their thanksgiving prayer, they echo their ancestors' words: "Everything we need to live a good life is here on this Mother Earth."

SPEAKING UP FOR NATURE

The Hiawatha belt design adorns the Haudenosaunee Confederacy flag.

People from many nations of the world gathered in Brazil in 1992 to discuss how to keep Earth healthy. A group of Haudenosaunee people were among those who traveled there. They reminded everyone that taking care of Earth is the responsibility of all human beings.

Today the Haudenosaunee have organized themselves to take action. Each nation sends leaders and scientists to task force meetings. There they discuss environmental problems affecting their communities. They want to clean up chemicals pouring out of factories and cities into rivers. They want to stop some mining, which can destroy forests and leak chemicals into nearby water. They want to prepare for rising temperatures that will affect plants, animals, and people.

TIMELINE

1142: Earliest date scholars place for the formation of the Haudenosaunee Confederacy of five nations. Other scholars place the date at 1451.

1613: Two Row Wampum treaty establishes relations between the Haudenosaunee and the Dutch.

1701: Haudenosaunee make peace with the English and the French, declaring neutrality.

1722: The Tuscarora join the Haudenosaunee Confederacy.

1754: The Albany Plan of Union is proposed at a meeting of colonists. It is Benjamin Franklin's plan for a central colonial government based on the Haudenosaunee example.

1794: Treaty of Canandaigua establishes peace between the United States and the Haudenosaunee.

1815: The Treaty of Ghent between Great Britain and the United States restores to Indian people the rights and treaties they had before 1811.

1924: The American Indian Citizen Act makes citizens of all American Indians. The Haudenosaunee decline U.S. citizenship in favor of retaining their nationhood.

1980: The Grand Council approves the initiation of the Iroquois Nationals lacrosse team. It competes against teams from around the world.

1987: In a special resolution, the U.S. Senate formally acknowledges the influence of the Haudenosaunee Great Law of Peace on the U.S. Constitution.

1989: New York museums return wampum belts to the Onondaga Nation.

2012: Kateri Tekakwitha (1656–1680) is declared the first American Indian saint by Pope Benedict XVI. She was a Mohawk–Algonquin woman who converted to Catholicism at 19.

2013: Two Row Wampum celebrates its 400th anniversary.

GLOSSARY

ally (AL-eye)—person, group, or country that helps and supports another

ancestor (AN-sess-tur)—family member who lived a long time ago

artisan (AR-tuh-zuhn)—skilled worker, especially one whose occupation requires hand skill

confederacy (kuhn-FE-druh-see)—union of people or groups with a common goal

democracy (di-MAH-kruh-see)—form of government in which the people elect their leaders

elder (EL-dur)—older person whose experience makes him or her a leader

province (PROV-uhnss)—defined region within Canada that has its own identity, but is still part of the larger country; similar to a U.S. state

reservation (rez-er-VAY-shuhn)—area of land set aside by the government for American Indians; in Canada reservations are called reserves

tradition (truh-DISH-uhn)—custom, idea, or belief passed down through time

READ MORE

Dolbear, Emily J., and Peter Benoit. *The Iroquois.*
New York: Children's Press, 2011.

Taylor, C.J. *Peace Walker.*
Plattsburgh, N.Y.: Tundra Books of Northern New York, 2014.

Yasuda, Anita. *Sky Woman and the Big Turtle: An Iroquois Creation Myth.* Minneapolis: Magic Wagon, 2012.

INTERNET SITES

FactHound offers a safe, fun way to find Internet sites related to this book. All of the sites on FactHound have been researched by our staff.

Here's all you do:

Visit *www.facthound.com*

Type in this code: 9781491449936

 Check out projects, games and lots more at
www.capstonekids.com

CRITICAL THINKING USING THE COMMON CORE

1. What if the Haudenosaunee had not agreed to work together as a confederacy? How would the lives of the Haudenosaunee people be different today? (Integration of Knowledge and Ideas)

2. Which historical time period or event do you think affected the lives of Haudenosaunee the most? Why? (Key Ideas and Details)

3. What do you think is the most important way that Haudenosaunee today protect their history for their children? Why? (Integration of Knowledge and Ideas)

INDEX